THE
TEMPLE VEIL TORN
IN TWO

The Ages of God

BOOK

MICHAEL SHENTON

The Ages of God: The Temple Veil was Torn in Two by Michael Shenton

This book is written to provide information and motivation to readers. Its purpose is not to render any type of psychological, legal, or professional advice of any kind. The content is the sole opinion and expression of the author, and not necessarily that of the publisher.

Copyright © 2022 by Michael Shenton

All rights reserved. No part of this book may be reproduced, transmitted, or distributed in any form by any means, including, but not limited to, recording, photocopying, or taking screenshots of parts of the book, without prior written permission from the author or the publisher. Brief quotations for noncommercial purposes, such as book reviews, permitted by Fair Use of the U.S. Copyright Law, are allowed without written permissions, as long as such quotations do not cause damage to the book's commercial value.

ISBN:978-1-951670-56-6 (Paperback)
ISBN:978-1-951670-55-9 (Digital)

Printed in the United States of America.

CONTENTS

INTRODUCTION V

CHAPTER 1 End of the "Old Covenant"—Start of the "New Covenant" 1

CHAPTER 2 End of Temple System—Start of Jesus / Holy Spirit Ministry 11

CHAPTER 3 End of the Law of Moses—Start of God's Law of Grace (Jesus fulfilled the Law) 23

CHAPTER 4 End of the Aaronic Priesthood—Start of the Melchizedek Priesthood (Jesus) 29

CHAPTER 5 End of the Lamb of Sacrifice each year Jesus, the once-only Sacrifice for Forgiveness of Sins 37

CHAPTER 6 End of High Priest placing Blood for Forgiveness of Sins on the mercy seat (Jesus' Blood is the once for all perfect sacrifice for the forgiveness of sins) 47

CHAPTER 7 End of High Priest Pronouncing forgiveness of sins thru Sacrifices (Belief in Jesus, his Blood, and Baptism is the only way to receive forgiveness of sins) ... 55

CHAPTER 8 End of Temple Priestly Rituals and Duties The Holy Spirit is now in charge of the church. 63

CHAPTER 9 End of the Earthly Holy Place We can enter the Heavenly Holy Place by the blood of Jesus. 73

CHAPTER 10 End of the High Priest as Mediator between Man and God (Believers now have direct access— The Holy Spirit dwells within us) 79

CHAPTER 11 End of Satan's reign Jesus took away the keys to death and hell. (From Satan) 85

CHAPTER 12 The way into Paradise the Garden of Eden has now been opened by Jesus (Believers are given a new spirit—they are a New Creation) 91

CHAPTER 13 Believers in Jesus have Everlasting Life They have passed out of Judgement 97

CHAPTER 14 The Simple Gift of Eternal Life 103

CHAPTER 15 Scriptures 111

CONCLUSION 117

BONUS 1: We are Called by God but come to a Comfortable Place we no Longer Obey God and Turn to Idols 127

BONUS 2: Putting our trust in a Man and not in God 130

ABOUT THE AUTHOR 137

INTRODUCTION

THE HOLY SPIRIT GAVE me the verses below at a Bible Study in Perth in September-2020.

The Holy Spirit then asked the question:

What was the meaning of "The Veil of the Temple was Torn in Two"?

I hope everyone understands that the Veil of the Temple was a very thick curtain that separated the Holy of Holies from the Main Court of the Temple.

> **Luke 23:44-46**
> ⁴⁴ Now it [l]was about the sixth hour, and there was darkness over

all the earth until the ninth hour. [45] Then the sun was [m]darkened, and the veil of the temple was torn in [n]two. [46] And when Jesus had cried out with a loud voice, He said, "Father, 'into your hands I commit my spirit.'" Having said this, He breathed his last.

Later, when thinking on this, I was given the verse below:

This verse proves that the Veil also represented the Flesh of Jesus.

Hebrews 10:19-22

[19] Therefore, brethren, having boldness[f] to enter the Holiest by the blood of Jesus, [20] by a new and living way which He consecrated for us, through the **veil, that is, his flesh**, [21] and *having* a High

Priest over the house of God, [22] let us draw near with a true heart in full assurance of faith, having our hearts sprinkled from an evil conscience and our bodies washed with pure water.

I then felt led to write this book on the subject of the **Temple Veil was Torn in Two**. The Summary below is trying to list all the meanings of the Temple Veil being torn in Two.

Summary:

- The Veil represents the Body and Flesh of Jesus being torn for us.
- End of the "Old Covenant"—Start of the "New Covenant"
- End of Temple System—Start of Jesus / Holy Spirit Ministry—Jesus completed his work

- End of the Law of Moses - Start of God's Law of Grace (Jesus fulfilled the Law)
- End of the Aaronic Priesthood—Start of the Melchizedek Priesthood (Jesus)
- (A change of Law results in a change in Priesthood)
- Aaronic Priesthood was human and temporary—Melchizedek Priesthood is spiritual and eternal
- End of Human High Priest who dies—Start of Jesus as the eternal High Priest
- End of Lamb of Sacrifice each year—Jesus is the once-only Sacrifice for Forgiveness of Sins
- Jesus' body is the Veil that was torn to forgive sins.
- End of High Priest placing Blood for Forgiveness of Sins on the mercy seat each year
- (Jesus' Blood is the once for all perfect sacrifice for the forgiveness of sins)

- End of High Priest Pronouncing forgiveness of sins thru Sacrifice of the Lamb
- (Belief in Jesus, his Blood, and Baptism is the only way to receive forgiveness of sins)
- End of Temple Priestly Rituals and Duties—Holy Spirit is now in charge of the church.
- End of the Earthly Holy Place—We can enter the Heavenly Holy Place by the blood of Jesus
- End of the High Priest as Mediator between Man and God
- (Believers now have direct access—The Holy Spirit dwells within us)
- (Our body is the Temple of the Holy Spirit)
- End of Satan's reign—Jesus took away the keys of death and hell

- (Jesus destroyed the works of Satan - gave us the power to defeat all the works of the enemy)
- Jesus has now opened the way into Paradise / Garden of Eden
- (Believers are given a new spirit—they are a New Creation)
- For those who believe in Jesus—Everlasting Life—we have passed out of Judgement
- Our Spirit is made alive and seated in Heavenly Places
- Jesus is King and Priest
- (Never before has these two Offices been held by one person—Jesus)
- Every person who believes in Jesus is given the right to be a Priest and King
- Circumcision Party tries to take believers back to the Temple System and the Law of Moses

- (If we try to become righteous by our works, we negate the Crucifixion of Jesus)
- Circumcision Party tries to control believers by applying the Law of Moses
- (They make themselves the Judge over believers, they replace God)
- Those that the Spirt of God leads are Sons of God
- Those that believe Jesus is the son of God are given the right to be a Child of God
- Those who the Holy Spirit leads are not under the Law
- Where there is no Law, there is no sin
- There is now no condemnation for those in Christ Jesus

After writing the summary, I started to explain as best I could the reasons and meaning why the Temple Veil was torn in two. So, I started researching the scriptures on the above summary items while trying to listen to the leading of the Holy Spirit.

These teachings follow when Jesus spoke to me face to face at a mine site and said he wanted to restore the True Gospel to the Church. Refer to my book:New Holy Spirit Age.

To briefly summarise, after a Shower, I was standing naked in my bathroom in January 2020. I felt liquid drops fall on my feet, and I looked down to see a pool of blood around my feet.

As I became concerned about what was happening, Jesus appeared in my bathroom/room and spoke to me audibly.

Jesus said he was disappointed with the Church and how they disrespected his crucifixion. He said they acted as if his crucifixion was not a big deal, and they had no idea of the pain, trauma, and suffering he went through that he might become the sacrifice for the forgiveness of sins for the whole world.

Jesus said most churches were preaching a False Gospel, Jesus said he sent me to restore the True Gospel to the Churches.

This book is part of restoring the True and Full Gospel message.

We must understand the Full Revelation of the Death, Crucifixion, and Resurrection of the Lord Jesus Christ.

The veil represents the body of Jesus which was torn for us. We are sanctified by the blood of Jesus. We are made holy and righteous by the blood of Jesus. Paul said we need to go forward being sanctified by Jesus. We cannot sanctify ourselves or work to make ourselves Holy and Righteous.

No man can be made Holy by the works of the Law. Anyone who is under the Law is under a curse.

Any gospel that does not recognize Jesus as the only way to the Father is a false Gospel.

The church needs to focus on Jesus and not on rituals, traditions, priests, and trying to make themselves Holy and Righteous. In the Book of Galatians, the Circumcision Party focused on these things, and Paul called it a "False Gospel."

A False Religion worships or exalts something above the authority of God. For example, if you worship the church, you attend and would prefer to obey the church elders rather than obey the Holy Spirit, then this is a False Religion.

If you worship the Bible and exalt the Bible above God, then this is a False Religion. The Bible cannot be more important than God. The Bible is a record of everything God has said and done, and the record cannot be greater than the God who gave the record. Sadly many Christians are not willing to listen to the Holy Spirit and obey the Holy Spirit but are willing to obey the Bible (or the person's interpretation of what the Bible says)

Every Sunday, in their church services, I hear Christians read from the Bible and say this is the Word of God. Only Jesus is "The Word of God";

anything representing itself as "The Word of God" is an idol and False Religion.

I understand that many Christians will disagree with what I have just said. That is because their Church is their God, and Satan has deceived them into a False Gospel. The Bible is a record for our understanding of what God has said or done, and it is not equal to Jesus.

Satan is very cunning, he presents something plausible and appears to be the truth, but it is not the truth. Anything like the truth but not the truth is a lie. Jesus said, "I am the Way, the truth and the life; there is no other way to the Father except through me."

The church needs to focus on Jesus; anything raised above the position of Jesus is Idolatry, and idolatry is raising anything above God and the Lord Jesus Christ. This applies to Pentecostal Churches as well as Mainline Churches.

The church needs to focus on Jesus and not on "The Communion," reading the Bible, having a sermon, or repenting and pronouncing forgiveness of sins. Even the Worship Team can become an Idol if the music becomes more important than Jesus. Where a church exalts these above Jesus, the church is operating in Idolatry.

I repeat the church needs to focus on Jesus. In the first church, the Lord's Supper was after the meeting. After the meeting, the people came together for a meal and celebrated the Lord's Death and Resurrection (Communion). Jesus, instruction was to remember his death and resurrection every day when you have a meal, not to make a ritual out of "The Communion" once on a Sunday.

I am not saying you should not have communion; the Holy Spirit must lead the reason to have the communion. I had communion as a family meal after the church service is preferable.

If Communion takes place because it is a ritual and is always done this way every Sunday, then we are not being led by the Holy Spirit and are in Idolatry.

In the new covenant, everyone is ordained into a Ministry by Jesus, Priests ordained by a Church Structure are not more qualified than anyone else.

So, where a church teaches that only a priest can sanctify the elements of the communion, This is old covenant temple worship, which was installed in the church by the Circumcision Party.

The Circumcision Party was a group of people from the Temple System who became believers in Jesus but missed their Temple Positions and the esteem they had in the community. They taught that belief in Jesus was not good enough; you had to be circumcised and obey the Law of Moses.

The Priests in the Circumcision Party then elevated themselves above the normal members of the congregation and above anyone that Jesus had called. Any church or Church Leader who teaches that you have to be Circumcised or Obey the Law of Moses is teaching a False Gospel.

The Torn Veil represents that the way into the Holy of Holies is available to every believer thru the Blood of Jesus.

No longer does a priest have to stand as an intermediary between God and Man. Now we have the Holy Spirit living in our hearts. The Holy Spirit is our intermediary, and the Holy Spirit is our Teacher, Guide, and Counsellor and will lead us into all Truth.

The best thing that came out of COVID and zooms church meetings was the focus had to be on Jesus and not on Church Traditions or having communion as a ceremony or ritual.

CHAPTER 1

END OF THE "OLD COVENANT"— START OF THE "NEW COVENANT"

God made several Covenants with people over the years: Noah, Abraham, Isaac, Jacob, Moses, and Israel, David, other Kings of Israel.

The last major covenant was called "The Covenant with the Children of Israel" and was also known as the Old Covenant. This can also be called the Covenant of Moses.

It was also contained in a book called the Book of the Covenant.

> **2 Chronicles 34:30**
> The king went up to the house of the Lord with all the men of Judah and the inhabitants of Jerusalem—the priests and the Levites, and all the people, great and small. And he read in their hearing all the words of the **Book of the Covenant** which had been found in the house of the Lord.

The Book of the Covenant contained all the laws, rules, and regulations (Ordinances) that the children of Israel had to obey to make themselves acceptable to God. This included the annual sacrifice of the Lamb for the Forgiveness of the Sins of Israel.

God's name in each covenant was different. The laws, rules, and regulations in each covenant were different. The early covenants did not have a priesthood. The last Old Covenant had a Priesthood of Aaron (and Levites) Moses was the Prophet and leader of Israel. And God said I would raise for you one like Moses, and you shall obey him in everything he says. This one, like Moses, was Jesus.

It was God's purpose to replace the Old Covenant with a New Covenant. Jesus was the start of the New Covenant. God planned that the New Covenant would operate thru Jesus.

Jesus is the author of a New Covenant not made with the blood of lambs but with the blood of Jesus, the Son of God. An eternal Covenant, an eternal inheritance, made with a new eternal priest after the Order of Melchizedek.

A New Covenant required a new Order of Priesthood. The Old Covenant was the Aaronic Priesthood.

The New Covenant was Jesus, a Priest after the order of Melchizedek. An everlasting covenant.

This is the New Covenant:I will put my law in their minds and write it on their [I]hearts, and I will be their God, and they shall be my people.

I will forgive their iniquity, and their sin I will remember no more.

In the Old Covenant, we were made Righteous and Holy by obeying the Law of Moses. In the New Covenant, we are made Righteous and Holy by believing that Jesus is the Son of God, and it is Jesus' Blood and Sacrifice that makes us Holy and acceptable to God. God was reconciling us to himself through his Son Jesus.

In the New Covenant, God, Himself comes and dwells in our Hearts. Christianity is the only religion where God comes and dwells in the hearts of the believers. We invite Jesus into our Hearts—he does not force himself upon us.

REFERENCES

Jeremiah 31:31-34

³¹ "Behold, the days are coming, says the Lord, when I will make a new covenant with the house of Israel and with the house of Judah — ³² not according to the covenant that I made with their fathers in the day *that* I took them by the hand to lead them out of the land of Egypt, my covenant which they broke, [h]though I was a husband to them, says the Lord. ³³ But this *is* the covenant that I will make with the house of Israel after those days, says the Lord:I will put my law in their minds and write it on their [I]hearts; I will be their God, and they shall be my people.

³⁴ No more shall every man teach his neighbor, and every man his brother, saying, 'Know the Lord,' for they all shall know Me, from the least to the greatest of them, says the Lord. "For I will forgive their iniquity, and their sin I will remember no more.

Mathew 26:28

For this is My blood of the New Covenant, which is shed for many for the remission of sins. This New Covenant is eternal; Jesus was the once for all sacrifice to forgive sins. And having been perfected, he became the author of eternal salvation to all who obey him, called by God as High Priest after the Oder of Melchizedek. (Eternal Priesthood).

John 3:15-17

Moses lifted the serpent in the wilderness; even so, the Son of Man must be lifted, ¹⁵ that whoever believes in Him should [c]not perish but have eternal life. ¹⁶ For God so loved the world that he gave his only begotten Son, that whoever believes in Him should not perish but have everlasting life. ¹⁷ For God did not send his Son into the world to condemn the world, but that the world through Him might be saved. ¹⁸ "He who believes in Him is not condemned; but he who does not believe is condemned already, because he has not believed in the name of the only begotten Son of God.

Hebrews 9:11-15

[11] But Christ came *as* High Priest of the good things [c]to come, with the greater and more perfect tabernacle not made with hands, that is, not of this creation. [12] Not with the blood of goats and calves, but with His blood, He entered the Most Holy Place once and for all, having obtained eternal redemption. [13] For if the blood of bulls and goats and the ashes of a heifer, sprinkling the unclean, [d]sanctifies for the [e]purifying of the flesh, [14] how much more shall the blood of Christ, who through the eternal Spirit offered Himself without [f]spot to God, cleanse your conscience from dead works to serve the living God? [15] And for this reason, He is the Mediator of the new covenant, using his death

to redeem the transgressions under the first covenant so that those who are called may receive the promise of eternal inheritance.

CHAPTER 2

End of Temple System—Start of Jesus / Holy Spirit Ministry—

The Veil of the Temple being torn in two represented the end of the Temple System. Jesus prophesied that the Temple system was coming to an end; he predicted the destruction of the Temple and the destruction of the Nation of Israel.

Jesus also predicted The Father would send the Holy Spirit in Jesus' place to be our teacher, guide, and counselor and to empower us to carry out the works and ministry of Jesus and to speak his words to people.

Jesus was to be crucified, dead, and buried on the third day rise from the dead. Jesus was then to ascend to heaven, and then Jesus would send the Holy Spirit to continue Jesus' ministry on the Earth. (In this age, Jesus is the name of the Father. Jesus is the name of the Son; Jesus is the name of the Holy Spirit)

The Holy Spirit is to be our Teacher, Guide, and Councillor. We do not need to be concerned about what we will speak, and the Holy Spirit will give us the words to say. Paul received the Gospel Message by Divine Revelation; he did not receive the Gospel Message by being taught by another person.

The work of Jesus thru the Holy Spirit is to empower us to carry out the works of Jesus. The Holy Spirit gives us Gifts and Power so we can speak Jesus' words and carry out the works and deeds of Jesus.

Jesus and Paul's ministry was not with wise and persuasive words but with a demonstration of God's Power with Miracles, Healings, and casting out demons.

Christians today should believe in God based on God's Power—not on Men's Wisdom.

Jesus said to wait until you receive Power from on High. For the first disciples, the power came on the day of Pentecost. When we are filled with the Holy Spirit, we receive Power from on High. In the church today, this is to take place by laying hands, just as Paul laid his hands on Timothy.

The believer's work today is by service, not by being a Priest or having a Position of Authority even though we are called to be Priests and Kings. If we read Paul's account of how a church should function, one person has a Psalm, another a Song, another a Teaching, or another a Prophesy; every believer should be able to contribute in turn to the meeting; it should not be one professional running everything.

Many Apostolic and Mainline Churches say you cannot do any of these things above unless you have a degree in Theology or a Certificate from the Bishop. This is a False Gospel and would instantly disqualify the first Apostles from carrying out any ministry in the Church.

This is the accusation the High Priest and the Leaders of the Temple wanted to make against Peter and John. They said Peter and John were uneducated and untrained men, so they marveled and realized they had been with Jesus. So, when Satan wants to stop a ministry being led by the Holy Spirit, this is his first accusation—Your Doctrine is incorrect because you have not been trained and do not have a Degree in Theology.

REFERENCES

Luke 21:5-28
Jesus Predicts the Destruction of the Temple

Then, as some spoke of the temple, how it was [c]adorned with beautiful stones and donations, He said, **6** "These things which you see—the days will come in which not *one* stone shall be left upon another that shall not be thrown down."

The Signs of the Times and the End of the Age

7 So they asked Him, saying, "Teacher, but when will these things be? And what sign *will there be* when these things are about to take place?" **8** And He said: "Take heed that you not be deceived. For many will come in My name, saying, 'I am *He*,' and, 'The time has drawn near.' [d]Therefore, do not [e]go after them. **9** But when you hear of wars and commotions, do not be terrified; for these things must come to pass first, but the end *will* not *come* immediately." **10** Then He said to them, "Nation will rise against nation and kingdom against kingdom. **11** And there will be great earthquakes in various places, and famines and pestilences; and there will be fearful sights and great signs from heaven. **12** But before all these things, they will lay their hands on you and persecute *you,* delivering *you* up to the synagogues and prisons. You will be brought before kings and rulers for My name's sake. ¹³ But it will turn out for you as an occasion for testimony. ¹⁴ Therefore settle *it* in your hearts not to meditate beforehand on what you will [f]answer; ¹⁵ for I will give you a mouth and wisdom which all your adversaries will not be able to contradict or [g]resist. ¹⁶ You will be betrayed even by parents and brothers, relatives and friends, and they will put *some* of you to death. ¹⁷ And you will be hated by all for My name's sake. ¹⁸ But not a hair of your head shall be lost. ¹⁹ By your patience, possess your souls.

The Destruction of Jerusalem

²⁰ "But when you see Jerusalem surrounded by armies, then know that its desolation is near. ²¹ Then let those who are in Judea flee to

the mountains, let those who are amid her depart, and let not those who are in the country enter her. ²² For these are the days of vengeance that all things which are written may be fulfilled. ²³ But woe to those who are pregnant and to those who are nursing babies in those days! For there will be great distress in the land and wrath upon this people. ²⁴ And they will fall by the edge of the sword and be led away captive into all nations. And Jerusalem will be trampled by Gentiles until the times of the Gentiles are fulfilled.

The Coming of the Son of Man
²⁵ "And there will be signs in the sun, in the moon, and the stars; and on the earth distress of nations, with perplexity, the sea and the

waves roaring; ²⁶ men's failing them from fear and the expectation of those things which are coming on the earth, for the powers of the heavens will be shaken. ²⁷ Then they will see the Son of Man coming in a cloud with power and great glory. ²⁸ Now when these things begin to happen, look up and lift your heads, because your redemption draws near.

John 16:5-15

⁵ "But now I go away to Him who sent me, and none of you asks me, 'Where are You going?' ⁶ But because I have said these things to you, sorrow has filled your heart. ⁷ Nevertheless, I tell you the truth. It is to your advantage that I go away; for if I do not go away, the Helper will not come to you; but

if I depart, I will send Him to you. **8** And when he has come, He will convict the world of sin, and righteousness, and judgment:**9** of sin, because they do not believe in Me; **10** of righteousness, because I go to My Father and you see me no more; **11** of judgment, because the ruler of this world is judged. **12** "I still have many things to say to you, but you cannot bear *them* now. **13** However, when He, the Spirit of truth, has come, He will guide you into all truth; for He will not speak on His *authority,* but whatever He hears He will speak, and He will tell you things to come. **14** He will glorify Me, for He will take of what is Mine and declare *it* to you. **15** All things that the Father has are Mine. Therefore

I said that He [c]will take of Mine and declare *it* to you.

Acts 1:4-8

⁴ And being assembled with *them,* He commanded them not to depart from Jerusalem, but to wait for the Promise of the Father, "which," *He said,* "you have heard from Me; ⁵ for John truly baptized with water, but you shall be baptized with the Holy Spirit not many days from now." ⁶ Therefore, when they had come together, they asked Him, saying, "Lord, will You at this time restore the kingdom to Israel?" ⁷ And He said to them, "It is not for you to know times or seasons which the Father has put in His authority. ⁸ But you shall receive power when the Holy Spirit has come upon you, and you shall be

[c]witnesses to Me in Jerusalem, and in all Judea and Samaria, and to the end of the earth."

CHAPTER 3

End of the Law of Moses— Start of God's Law of Grace (Jesus fulfilled the Law)

It should be noted that the scribes and Pharisees of the Temple did not like John the Baptist because he did not conform to the Temple rules and regulations for the forgiveness of sins. John the Baptist was a prophet sent from God; the Temple Leadership refused to believe in John even though all the people believed that John was a prophet and went to John to be baptized in water to forgive sins.

The scribes and Pharisees did not like Jesus and complained that Jesus did not obey the Law of Moses or the Temple's rules and regulations. The Temple Leadership decided that anyone who acknowledged that Jesus was the Christ would be put out of the Temple even though many people did believe Jesus was the Christ or a at least a Prophet.

The Law of Moses was a system where you could try and obtain God's grace and mercy by obeying the Law, rules, and regulations, and by the Priest being the Intermediary between man and God. Once a year, The Priest offered the Lamb as a sacrifice for sins, and the Priest announced the Forgiveness of Sins to the people. When Jesus came, it was the start of receiving God's grace and mercy through belief in Jesus as the Son of God.

By believing in Jesus as the Son of God, we have the right to become a "Child of God." Jesus said that when people believed he was the Son of

God, then they would receive the gift of eternal life and the Right (or Power) to become a Child of God.

When we believe in Jesus, we are no longer under the Law. Jesus has given us the right to be a new spiritual being, a heavenly spiritual being with the right to be seated in heavenly places in Christ Jesus.

This is a gift. You cannot earn a gift, nor can you lose it because it is given with "Unconditional Love" we have received the gift by Grace.

We have been saved by God's grace and not by our works or righteousness.

When Jesus purged us of our sins, he sat down at the Father's right hand.

Jesus is the mediator of a New Covenant, much better than the Covenant obtained under the Law of Moses. This New Covenant is eternal and unchanging and will never end. Truly God's grace is amazing that thru the Blood of Jesus, God forgives all our sins and remembers them no more. This is the Law of God's Grace; you cannot earn God's Grace by carrying out the works of the Law. Jesus' Sacrifice sanctifies us and makes us holy and righteous.

If we try to obey the Laws of Moses to sanctify ourselves and make ourselves holy and righteous, then we nullify the work of Christ and die in our sins. No person is justified under the Law of Moses, it is impossible to keep and obey all the laws, and therefore we cannot obtain righteousness under the Law of Moses. We are trying to obtain righteousness by works instead of obtaining righteousness by faith in Jesus.

REFERENCES

John 3:16
¹⁴ And as Moses lifted the serpent in the wilderness, even so, must the Son of Man be lifted, ¹⁵ that whoever believes in Him should [c]not perish but have eternal life. ¹⁶ For God so loved the world that He gave His only begotten Son, that **whoever believes in Him** should not perish but have everlasting life. ¹⁷ For God did not send His Son into the world to condemn the world, but that the world through Him might be saved.

John 1:10-13
¹⁰ He was in the world, and the world was made through Him, and

the world did not know Him. [11] He came to His [c]own, and His [d] own did not receive Him. [12] But as many as received Him, to them He gave the [e]right to **become children of God**, to those who believe in His name: [13] who were born, not of blood, nor the will of the flesh, nor the will of man, but God.

Hebrews 8:10 & 12
[10] For this *is* the covenant that I will make with the house of Israel after those days, says the Lord: I will put My laws in their mind and write them on their hearts, and I will be their God, and they shall be My people. [12] For I will be merciful to their unrighteousness, and their sins [b]**and their lawless deeds I will remember no more."**

CHAPTER 4

End of the Aaronic Priesthood—Start of the Melchizedek Priesthood (Jesus)

When the Veil was torn in two, this symbolized a change in Priesthood.

Where there is a change in the law, there is a change in the priesthood. (Hebrews 6:12)

The Aaronic Priesthood served the Law of Moses. The Melchizedek Priesthood serves the Law of the Grace of God. Jesus is the High Priest of the Melchizedek Priesthood. This Melchizedek

Priesthood is extremely important as Paul mentions it 7 or 8 times in the Book of Hebrews.

The Aaronic Priesthood is Earthly and Temporary. The Melchizedek Priesthood is Heavenly and Eternal.

The Tabernacle of Moses was a shadow, copy, and image of the Heavenly Tabernacle. This Earthly Tabernacle was inferior to the Heavenly Tabernacle. The Aaronic Priesthood was temporary because the High Priest died and had to be replaced.

The Aaronic Priesthood offered the blood of lambs and needed rituals to enter the Holy Place. Then once a year, the High Priest announced forgiveness of sins for the nation of Israel.

The tearing of the veil in two as the end of the Aaronic Priesthood was further emphasized when some 40 years later, the Temple was destroyed so that not one stone remained one upon another.

God declared that the Temple Worship System and the Aaronic Priesthood were destroyed and would never be resurrected. God showed that there was now a New Covenant, a new system. God made sure there was no way for the Sacrifice of Lambs to continue in the New Covenant. Even today, the Jews cannot sacrifice Lambs for the Forgiveness of Sins. For without the shedding of blood, there is no forgiveness of sins.

The Melchizedek Priesthood is eternal. Only a Heavenly Spiritual being could be a Priest of the Order of the Melchizedek Priesthood, and Jesus fulfilled this requirement of the Melchizedek Priesthood.

It then goes on to say that whoever believes in Jesus is a Priest and a King. Therefore every believer is a Priest after the Order of Melchizedek.

Every believer in Jesus is a new Spiritual Being, an Eternal New Creation.

The Temple Priesthood is the old covenant and is finished with the Temple's destruction. Its End was signified by the Veil of the Temple being split from Top to Bottom. Christians no longer need a Priest to stand between them and God in them, the Holy Spirit.

Christians no longer need a Priest to minister the Law to them. For those who the Spirit of God leads, there is no longer any law. We have passed out of the Condemnation of the Law, entered into the Grace of Eternal Life, and are immediately made Holy by the Blood of Jesus, not by our Righteousness. Our Spirit is made Holy, Righteous, and Sanctified by the Blood of Jesus.

REFERENCES

Hebrews 7:11-17

[11] Therefore, if perfection were through the Levitical priesthood (for under it, the people received the law), what further need *was there* that another priest should rise according to the order of Melchizedek and not be called according to the order of Aaron? [12] For the priesthood being changed, there is also a change of the law. [13] For He of whom these things are spoken belongs to another tribe, from which no man has [b]officiated at the altar. [14] For *it is* evident that our Lord arose from Judah, of which tribe Moses spoke nothing concerning [c]priesthood. [15]

And it is yet far more evident if, in the likeness of Melchizedek, there arises another priest [16] who has come, not according to the law of a fleshly commandment, but according to the power of an endless life. [17] For [d], He testifies: "You *are* a priest forever. According to the order of Melchizedek."

Acts 26:17-18
Paul Recounts His Conversion

[17] I will [b]deliver you from the *Jewish* people, as well as *from* the Gentiles, to whom I [c]now send you, [18] to open their eyes, to turn *them* from darkness to light, and *from* the power of Satan to God, that they may receive forgiveness of sins and an inheritance among those who are **sanctified**[d] by faith in Me.'

Romans 8:11
But if the Spirit of Him who raised Jesus from the dead dwells **in you**, He who raised **Christ** from the dead will also give life to **you**r mortal bodies through His Spirit who dwells **in you**.

CHAPTER 5

END OF THE LAMB OF SACRIFICE EACH YEAR JESUS, THE ONCE-ONLY SACRIFICE FOR FORGIVENESS OF SINS

UNDER THE LAW OF Moses, the High Priest was ordained to offer sacrifices and blood for the forgiveness of sin.

Once a year, the High Priest entered the Holy of Holies alone, took the blood of the sacrifice with him, and offered the blood for the forgiveness of his sin and the sin of the people of Israel.

The High Priest was ministering daily and repeatedly offering the same sacrifices for the forgiveness of sin. It was not a once for all eternal sacrifice but had to be continually repeated each year.

Before the High Priest could enter the Holy of Holies, he had to be descended from a certain priestly family, dedicated to God, sanctified with rituals and made ready, being washed, wearing special clothes, wearing a plate engraved with "Holiness to the Lord," and anointed with oil.

They were not allowed to enter the Holy of Holies until they had been consecrated. If they tried to enter the Holy Place without going thru the correct consecrating procedure, they died. The animals were killed, and the blood was used to consecrate the Altar, the Priests, and their garments. For seven days, the atonement/sanctification continued, and the priest's clothes were also sprinkled with the blood of the sacrifices.

The Priest was then able to enter the Holy of Holies and place the blood on the mercy seat of the Ark of the Covenant. The Priest's Final Act was to pronounce that the Sins of the People had now been forgiven.

This Aaronic High Priest was a temporary Priest whose duties were carried out on the earth and not eternal being interrupted by the priest's death. This forgiveness of sins only lasted for one year.

When Jesus was crucified, dead and buried, and raised from the Dead, Jesus entered the Tabernacle and Holy of Holies in Heaven to make final atonement for the sins of the whole world and the pronouncement for the forgiveness of sins as an eternal covenant forever by being the Eternal Priest in the Order of Melchizedek. This covenant was eternal and could never be broken because the covenant was confirmed with an oath sworn by God himself, and an eternal High Priest carried out duties.

Jesus entered the Heavenly Tabernacle once and for all to offer his body and blood as a sacrifice to forgive sins. Jesus will never die again or be sacrificed for our sins. Jesus said it was finished just before he died on the cross. The sacrifice of Jesus for the forgiveness of sins was completed at the cross. Jesus still had to descend into Death and Hell, be raised from the dead, and ascend to the Right Hand of God the Father.

REFERENCES

Exodus 28:1-4

28 "Now take Aaron your brother, and his sons with him, from among the children of Israel, that he may minister to Me as a priest, Aaron *and* Aaron's sons:Nadab, Abihu, Eleazar, and Thamar. 2 And you shall make [a]holy garments for Aaron your brother, for glory and beauty. 3 So you shall speak to all gifted artisans, whom I have filled with the spirit of wisdom, that they may make Aaron's garments, to consecrate him, that he may minister to Me as a priest.

4 And these *are* the garments which they shall make:a breastplate, an [b]ephod, a robe, a skillfully

woven tunic, a turban, and a sash. So they shall make holy garments for Aaron your brother and his sons, that he may minister to Me as a priest.

Exodus 29:1-9
Aaron and His Sons Consecrated
²⁹ "And this is what you shall do to them to hallow them for ministering to Me as priests: Take one young bull and two rams without blemish, ² and unleavened bread, unleavened cakes mixed with oil, and unleavened wafers anointed with oil (you shall make them of wheat flour). ³ You shall put them in one basket and bring them in the basket, with the bull and the two rams. ⁴ "And Aaron and his sons you shall bring to the door of the tabernacle of meeting, and

you shall wash them with water. **5** Then you shall take the garments, put the tunic on Aaron, and the robe of the ephod, the ephod, and the breastplate, and gird him with the intricately woven band of the ephod. **6** You shall put the turban on his head and the holy crown on the turban. **7** And you shall take the anointing oil, pour *it* on his head, and anoint him. **8** Then you shall bring his sons and put tunics on them. **9** And you shall gird them with sashes, Aaron and his sons, and put the hats on them. The priesthood shall be theirs for a perpetual statute. So, you shall consecrate Aaron and his sons.

Hebrews 10:11
Christ's Death Perfects the Sanctified

¹¹ And every priest stands ministering daily and repeatedly offering the same sacrifices, which can never take away sins. ¹² But this Man, after He had offered one sacrifice for sins forever, sat down at the right hand of God, ¹³ from that time waiting till His enemies are made His footstool. ¹⁴ For by one offering, He has perfected forever those who are being [d]sanctified.

Hebrews 9:11-15
Heavenly Sanctuary

¹¹ But Christ came *as* High Priest of the good things [c]to come, with the greater and more perfect tabernacle not made with hands, that is, not of this creation. ¹² Not with the blood of goats and calves, but with His blood, He entered the

Most Holy Place once for all, having obtained eternal redemption.

¹³ For if the blood of bulls and goats and the ashes of a heifer, sprinkling the unclean, [d]sanctifies for the [e]purifying of the flesh, ¹⁴ how much more shall the blood of Christ, who through the eternal Spirit offered Himself without [f] spot to God, cleanse your conscience from dead works to serve the living God? ¹⁵ And for this reason He is the Mediator of the new covenant, using death, for the redemption of the transgressions under the first covenant, that those who are called may receive the promise of the eternal inheritance.

CHAPTER 6

End of High Priest placing Blood for Forgiveness of Sins on the mercy seat (Jesus' Blood is the once for all perfect sacrifice for the forgiveness of sins)

THE PRIEST OF THE Aaronic Priesthood in the Temple was to enter the Holy of Holies and then place the blood on the mercy seat on the Ark of the Covenant between the two cherubim.

The Mercy Seat represented the actual meeting place between God and Man. Therefore it had to be sanctified and made Holy by the Blood of the Sacrifice. All utensils in the Temple used in connection with God had to be sanctified by being daubed with the sacrifice's blood, including the Altar.

When Jesus died, his blood now sanctified the place in heaven where God would meet with his people. (In the Heavenly Tabernacle)

Just as there was a Heavenly Tabernacle, Moses was told to make an Earthly Copy of the Heavenly Tabernacle, and this earthly copy eventually became the Temple. The Temple represented the earthly copy of the Heavenly Tabernacle.

However, when Jesus died, the earthly copy, the Temple at Jerusalem, was destroyed, and the Veil in the Temple was destroyed.

Our body now became the Earthly Temple in which God would dwell. The Holy Spirit came and dwelled in our hearts. Our Hearts became where God is dwelling and speaking to us through the Holy Spirit.

As our body is the Temple of the Holy Spirit, our hearts have been sanctified by the blood of Jesus so that we may meet with God through the Ministry of the Holy Spirit. This place of the meeting and mercy seat on earth is now in the heart of every believer.

Jesus said my sheep know my voice; therefore, every believer should now hear the voice of the Holy Spirit speaking to them and giving them guidance and direction in their lives. However, many people find it hard to hear the voice of the Holy Spirit, The Holy Spirit speaks like a small quiet voice in our minds. Most believers dismiss this small quiet voice because they believe it is their voice.

Everything in the new covenant is received by faith. If you believe the Holy Spirit will speak to you, he WILL. If you believe the Holy Spirit will not speak to you, he WILL NOT.

If you believe God will speak to you but have difficulty hearing his voice, you need to create a relationship.

Think of an earthly relationship as a Husband and Wife. If the Husband does not have a close relationship with his wife, then the Husband has trouble hearing from and understanding the Wife, and eventually, the two will drift apart. So, it is with our relationship with God. If we have not spent time with the Holy Spirit and have not cultivated a close relationship with the Holy Spirit, then we will have trouble hearing from and understanding the Holy Spirit.

In the earthly realm, everything gets better with practice. Therefore, we need to practice speaking to God and hearing from God. As we practice speaking to God, our relationship with God will strengthen, our faith will increase, and our hearing from God will become easier and easier.

REFERENCES

Leviticus 16:1-2
The Mercy Seat
¹⁶ Now the Lord spoke to Moses after the death of the two sons of Aaron, when they offered *profane fire* before the Lord and died; ² and the Lord said to Moses: "Tell Aaron your brother not to come at *just* any time into the Holy *Place* inside the veil, before the mercy seat which *is* on the ark, lest he die; for I will appear in the cloud above the mercy seat.

Hebrews 9:1-10
The Earthly Sanctuary
⁹ Then indeed, even the first *covenant* had ordinances of divine

service and the earthly sanctuary. [2] For a tabernacle was prepared: the first *part,* in which *was* the lampstand, the table, and the showbread, which is called the [a]sanctuary; [3] and behind the second veil, the part of the tabernacle which is called the Holiest of All, [4] which had the golden censer and the ark of the covenant overlaid on all sides with gold, in which *were* the golden pot that had the manna, Aaron's rod that budded, and the tablets of the covenant; [5] and above it were the cherubim of glory overshadowing the mercy seat. Of these things, we cannot now speak in detail.

Limitations of the Earthly Service

⁶ Now, when these things had been thus prepared, the priests went into the tabernacle's first part, performing the services. ⁷ But into the second part, the high priest went alone once a year, not without blood, which he offered for himself and the people's sins committed in ignorance; ⁸ the Holy Spirit indicating this, that the way into the Holiest of All was not yet made manifest while the first tabernacle was still standing. ⁹ It was symbolic for the present time in which both gifts and sacrifices are offered, which cannot make him who performed the service perfect

regarding the conscience— [10] concerned only with foods and drinks, various washings, and fleshly ordinances imposed until the time of reformation.

CHAPTER 7

End of High Priest Pronouncing forgiveness of sins thru Sacrifices (Belief in Jesus, his Blood, and Baptism is the only way to receive forgiveness of sins)

In the Temple system, the Priest was responsible for the sacrifice to forgive sins. The priest would carry out the act of Atonement for the people's sins. When the priest had completed the atonement, he would then pronounce the person was clean.

This represented the priest saying that the person's sin had been forgiven. The person could not become clean unless the priest had carried out the sacrifice and atonement, and the priest inspected them to ensure they were clean.

When Jesus died on the cross, Jesus was the once and for all perfect sacrifice for the forgiveness of all sins, past, present, and future.

After the sacrifice of Jesus, there will no longer be any more sacrifices offered for sins because Jesus' work was completed on the cross.

Jesus' work was twofold, Jesus was sacrificed on the Earth, and his blood cleansed the Earth and Mankind. Jesus entered the Holy of Holies and presented his sacrifice and blood there. The earthly veil of the Temple was torn in two to represent the way into the Holy of Holies has now been opened by the blood of Jesus so that we may approach the father.

That is why Paul said we are seated in Heavenly Places in Christ Jesus. When we believe in Jesus, we become a new creation, a new spiritual being. Therefore our spirit has access to the throne in heaven on which Jesus sits.

Therefore, if we are seated in Heavenly Places, we must be next to the throne in Heaven.

It is important to note that when we become a new creation that has never been seen before, it does not exist and then transforms into a different form of spiritual being or a different form of creation.

Paul further says that we have become Kings and Priests to God forever. We are seated in Heavenly Places in Christ Jesus.

Our Spirit Being is made Perfect, Holy, and Righteous. Our carnal self or Old Man needs to be perfected and sanctified, and we will not receive a new body until the Coming of Jesus.

Our Spirit is eternal and never dies; it is our body that dies. Jesus clearly states to fear God as God is the only one that can destroy an eternal

Spirit. No man, not even satan, can kill a man's spirit.

It is important to understand our full blessing, in Ephesians says that it is by Grace we have been saved, that we have been Pre-Destined, Called, Justified and Glorified. Do you know that you have been Glorified? What does that mean for you? We need to know the fullness of the Victory that Jesus won for us on the Cross.

REFERENCES

Hebrews 5:1-4
⁵ For every high priest taken from among men is appointed for men in things bout God, that he may offer both gifts and sacrifices for sins. ² He can [a]have compassion on those who are ignorant and going astray, since he is also subject to weakness. ³ Because of this, he is required as for the people, so also for himself, to offer *sacrifices* for sins. ⁴ And no man takes this honor to himself, but he who is called by God, just as Aaron *was*.

Ephesians 2:4-10
⁴ But God, who is rich in mercy, because of His great love with

which He loved us, ⁵ even when we were dead in trespasses, made us alive together with Christ (by grace you have been saved), ⁶ and raised *us* together, and made *us* sit together in the heavenly *places* in Christ Jesus, ⁷ that in the ages to come He might show the exceeding riches of His grace in *His* kindness toward us in Christ Jesus. ⁸ For by grace you have been saved through faith, and that not of yourselves; *it is* the gift of God, ⁹ not of works, lest anyone should boast. ¹⁰ For we are His workmanship, created in Christ Jesus for good works, which God prepared beforehand that we should walk in them.

Romans 8:28-30
²⁸ And we know that all things work together for good to those

who love God, to those who are the called according to *His* purpose. ²⁹ For whom He foreknew, He also predestined *to be* conformed to the image of His Son, that He might be the firstborn among many brethren. ³⁰ Moreover whom He predestined, these He also called; whom He called, these He also justified; and whom He justified, these He also glorified.

Romans 8:1-8
Free from Indwelling Sin

⁸ *There is* therefore now no condemnation to those who are in Christ Jesus, who[a] do not walk according to the flesh, but according to the Spirit. ² For the law of the Spirit of life in Christ Jesus has made me free from the law of sin and death. ³ For what the law could not do in

that it was weak through the flesh, God *did* by sending His own Son in the likeness of sinful flesh, on account of sin:He condemned sin in the flesh, [4] that the righteous requirement of the law might be fulfilled in us who do not walk according to the flesh but according to the Spirit. [5] For those who live according to the flesh set their minds on the things of the flesh, but those *who live* according to the Spirit, the things of the Spirit. [6] For to be [b]carnally minded *is* death, but to be spiritually minded *is* life and peace. [7] Because the [c] carnal mind *is* enmity against God; for it is not subject to the law of God, nor indeed can be. [8] So then, those who are in the flesh cannot please God.

CHAPTER 8

END OF TEMPLE PRIESTLY RITUALS AND DUTIES THE HOLY SPIRIT IS NOW IN CHARGE OF THE CHURCH.

When the Temple was destroyed, this signified that all the Priestly Duties on earth had ceased. It was interesting that the Ark of the Covenant also completely disappeared. So the priest could not carry out any priestly duties from the time of Jesus' Crucifixion up to the present day.

God has arranged things so that there are earthly copies of things in Heaven.

So, when Jesus ascended into heaven, he sent the Holy Spirit to the earth. The Holy Spirit is now God's representative on the Earth until Jesus' second coming. The Holy Spirit dwells in us and is the intermediary between God and us. God is dwelling in us thru the Holy Spirit. Our body has become the Temple of the Living God. God in us the Hope of Glory.

We have an intercessor or intermediary with direct communication with God. God the Father, Jesus, and the Holy Spirit are one. Therefore the communication between them is seamless.

So, as the Holy Spirit lives in all believers, the communication between the believer and God should also be seamless.

Not as in the old covenant where the intermediary was a High Priest with an imperfect connection with God, and it was so imperfect that a rope was tied around his angles in case he died in the Holy of Holies while trying to converse with

God. Even today, when a church elder or priest tries to be the mediator between the believer and God, this is the Old Covenant System, and the believer is right back in the bondage of the Temple System.

I find it interesting that Aaron's attempts at becoming a Priest were a bit of a disaster right at the beginning. First, he makes Golden Calf replace the God of Israel so that God eventually kills off the first generation that came out of Egypt. Then when Aaron and his sons carry out their Priestly duties at the Tabernacle before God, fire comes out of God for the first time and destroys Aarons's first sons, Nadab and Abihu, as they offered profane fire before the Lord. Then Moses gave other instructions to Aaron and his other two sons, Eleazar and Thamar. Still, they were so afraid of God killing them that they did not carry out Moses' instructions, and Moses became angry, eventually relented when he realized they were afraid.

In the first Church, the Holy Spirit was in charge. When Peter was on the Housetop praying, the Holy Spirit gave him a vision concerning unclean animals and told him that what was Unclean, God had now made clear. The Holy Spirit told Peter that three men were seeking him and that he would go with them, doubting Nothing. Peter went to Cornelius' Household, and the Holy Spirit fell on the uncircumcised people as Peter spoke to them.

Immediately after Peter returned to Jerusalem, those of the Circumcision Party contended with him and said that he went in and ate with uncircumcised people. These people were ex-Temple Priests who had converted to Christianity and believed the first Christians should obey the Law of Moses. They had seen the Holy Spirit fall on the Gentiles but still complained.

Now at the first church at Antioch, the Holy Spirit said, set apart for me Paul and Barnabas, for I have work for them to do. Then having fasted and prayed and laid hands on them, they sent out Paul and Barnabas, sent by the Holy Spirit.

There are many other examples of Paul, Phillip, and other people in the early church being instructed by the Holy Spirit to go to certain places or do certain things.

In the first Church meetings, the Holy Spirit directed the meetings, and each person spoke as the Holy Spirit directed them.

You see the same thing in the Welsh revival of 1904:the Holy Spirit directed the meetings, and people spoke, gave testimonies, prayed, or sang hymns as the Holy Spirit directed them.

REFERENCES

John 15:26-27

²⁶ "But when the [c]Helper comes, whom I shall send to you from the Father, the Spirit of truth who proceeds from the Father, He will testify of Me. ²⁷ And you also will bear witness, because you have been with Me from the beginning.

Acts 4:31

³¹ And when they had prayed, the place where they were assembled was shaken; and they were all filled with the Holy Spirit, and they spoke the word of God with boldness.

Acts 8:26-29

²⁶ Now an angel of the Lord spoke to Philip, saying, "Arise and go toward the south along the road which goes down from Jerusalem to Gaza." This is [e]desert. ²⁷ So, he arose and went. And behold, a man of Ethiopia, a eunuch of great authority under Candace the queen of the Ethiopians, who had charge of all her treasury, and had come to Jerusalem to worship, ²⁸ was returning. And sitting in his chariot, he was reading Isaiah the prophet. ²⁹ Then the Spirit said to Philip, "Go near and overtake this chariot."

Acts 9:10-17
Ananias Baptizes Saul

¹⁰ Now there was a certain disciple at Damascus named Ananias; and

to him, the Lord said in a vision, "Ananias." And he said, "Here I am, Lord." ¹¹ So the Lord *said* to him, "Arise and go to the street called Straight, and inquire at the house of Judas for *one* called Saul of Tarsus, for behold, he is praying. ¹² And in a vision, he has seen a man named Ananias coming in and putting *his* hand on him so that he might receive his sight."

¹³ Then Ananias answered, "Lord, I have heard from many about this man, how much [b]harm he has done to Your saints in Jerusalem. ¹⁴ And here he has authority from the chief priests to bind all who call on Your name." ¹⁵ But the Lord said to him, "Go, for he is a chosen vessel of Mine to bear My name before Gentiles, kings, and the children[c] of Israel. ¹⁶ For I

will show him how many things he must suffer for My name's sake."

¹⁷ And Ananias went his way and entered the house; and laying his hands on him, he said, "Brother Saul, the Lord [d]Jesus, who appeared to you on the road as you came, has sent me that you may receive your sight and be filled with the Holy Spirit." ¹⁸ Immediately, there fell from his eyes *something* like scales, and he received his sight at once, and he arose and was baptized.

CHAPTER 9

End of the Earthly Holy Place
We can enter the Heavenly Holy Place by the blood of Jesus

When Jesus died, the veil of the Temple was torn in two, and then the Temple itself was destroyed in about 70 AD.

So that was the end of the Earthly Holy Place at that time.

The blood of Jesus is the perfect sacrifice that allows us to enter the Heavenly Holy of Holies, the Tabernacle of God, which is in Heaven. This Heavenly Tabernacle with God was the blueprint for the Earthly Tabernacle, the copy Moses built.

As the earthly place was ended, so were the laws associated with the Earthly Place ended.

The Earthly Place / Temple was a copy of the Heavenly Tabernacle. So when Jesus died and offered his blood as the sacrifice for sin, he entered the Heavenly Holy Tabernacle and presented his blood as the once for all sacrifice.

Those who believe in Jesus have the right to enter the Heavenly Holy of Holies or Holy Place using the Blood of Jesus.

The Earthly Tabernacle is now represented by the body and heart of those that believe in Jesus. Paul said our body is the Temple of the Holy Spirit.

For those who believe in Jesus, the Holy Spirit came and fused with our Spirit and made us a new Spiritual Being, then the Holy Spirit came and dwelt in our Heart. The blood was used in the earthly tabernacle on the mercy seat of the

Ark of the Covenant to cleanse the mercy seat and sanctify the Meeting place of God and Man (The High Priest) so that when the High Priest met with God, he was not instantly killed because of his sinful nature.

So today, because of the Blood of Jesus, the Holy Spirit can dwell in the meeting place of our heart because the Blood of Jesus has sanctified this place so that God can meet us in our hearts and we are not instantly killed because of our sinful nature.

Our sinful nature has been removed by the Blood of Jesus, and we are now sanctified and made Holy and Righteous so that God can meet with us and his Holy nature does not destroy us.

In the Old covenant, when anyone who had not been sanctified came into the presence of God, Fire immediately came out from God and instantly killed them.

This is what happened to Aaron's sons (Eleazar and Thamar) when they approached God to offer incense which God had not commanded them (profane fire), so fire came out from the Lord and consumed them.

When Uzziah put out his hand to steady the Ark of the Covenant, the power came out from the Lord and killed him also.

When Priests came into the Holy of Holies and had not been correctly sanctified and made Holy, Power came out from the Ark of the Covenant and Killed them.

That is why the High Priest had a rope around his ankle so that if he died, the priests outside the Holy of Holies could pull the dead priest out of the Holy Place and back into the Temple area.

Therefore, we have now been made Holy and Righteous, so God dwells in our hearts, and we can speak directly to God without being killed or consumed by a Holy God.

REFERENCES

Philippians 2:8-11
And being found in appearance as a man, He humbled Himself and became obedient to *the point of* death, even the death of the cross. ⁹ Therefore, God also has highly exalted Him and given Him the name which is above every name, ¹⁰ that at the name of Jesus every knee should bow, of those in heaven, and those on earth, and those under the earth, ¹¹ and *that* every tongue should confess that Jesus Christ *is* Lord, to the glory of God the Father.

Hebrews 10:19-22

19 Therefore, brethren, having boldness[f] to enter the Holiest by the blood of Jesus, 20 by a new and living way which He consecrated for us, through the veil, that is, His flesh, 21 and *having* a High Priest over the house of God, 22 let us draw near with a true heart in full assurance of faith, having our hearts sprinkled from an evil conscience and our bodies washed with pure water.

CHAPTER 10

END OF THE HIGH PRIEST AS MEDIATOR BETWEEN MAN AND GOD (BELIEVERS NOW HAVE DIRECT ACCESS—THE HOLY SPIRIT DWELLS WITHIN US)

(OUR BODY IS THE Temple of the Holy Spirit)

In the Old Covenant, only Moses or Joshua or the High Priest could communicate directly with God and live.

At that time, the Prophet was the main intermediary between man and God and carried out all the instructions between man and God. The High Priest, as an intermediary, was mainly concerned with carrying out religious ceremonies and rituals and presenting sacrifices for sin.

Even in the Old Covenant, God wanted to speak directly to people, but they would not because they were too afraid. When God came down on Mount Sinai to speak to them, they were afraid and said let not God speak to us but speak to Moses, and we will listen to Moses.

Even in the Old Covenant, God wanted them to be a Nation of Priests and Kings, but they would not because they were afraid of God and unwilling to obey God.

Therefore, because they were afraid to speak to God directly in the Old Covenant, God allowed them to have the Intermediatory of Moses and Aaron, where God met with Moses and Aaron. Then they repeated what God had told them and spoke God's words to the people.

This was not God's plan, and the people lost favor with God and feared God. Even in the Old Covenant, God spoke to Moses and Joshua.

Even in the New Covenant, many Christians do not have a relationship with God, do not favor God, and have more faith in their church than they have in God.

Therefore, because of their unbelief, they have placed an intermediary between themselves and God and do not speak directly with God. Their God is their church, their God is the Priest, and their God is the Bible. Their intermediary has become their God.

They are putting other things before God, placing an Idol before God.

We must ensure that only God is first in our lives and everything else is a poor second. We were made to please God and not to please man or earthly priests or pastors.

We need to place our trust in God, and we need to obey the leading of the Holy Spirit.

Trying to please other people rather than obeying the Holy Spirit is not pleasing to God.

Trust in the Lord with all your heart, lean not on your understanding, in all your ways acknowledge God, and he will direct your paths.

Cursed is the man who puts his trust in men. You shall not make any other gods for yourselves; neither shall you bow down and serve them, for I am a jealous God and shall visit iniquity upon those that serve other gods.

REFERENCES

Exodus 20:18-21
The People Afraid of God's Presence

¹⁸ Now all the people witnessed the thundering, the lightning flashes, the sound of the trumpet, and the mountain smoking; and when the people saw *it,* they trembled and stood afar off. ¹⁹ Then they said to Moses, "You speak with us, and we will hear; but let not God speak with us, lest we die." ²⁰ And Moses said to the people, "Do not fear; for God has come to test you, and that His fear may be before you, so that you may not sin." ²¹ So the people stood afar off, but Moses

drew near the thick darkness where God *was*.

Jeremiah 17:5
Thus says the Lord:"**Cursed** is **the man** who trusts in **man** and makes flesh his strength, whose heart departs from the Lord.

Romans 8:14
For as many as are **led by the Spirit** of God, these are sons of God.

Galatians 5:18
But if you are **led by the Spirit**, you are not under the law.

CHAPTER 11

END OF SATAN'S REIGN JESUS TOOK AWAY THE KEYS TO DEATH AND HELL. (FROM SATAN)

(JESUS DESTROYED THE WORKS of Satan)

(Jesus gave us the power to defeat all the works of the enemy)

Jesus said he came to destroy the works of Satan.

The lame shall walk, the blind shall see, and the deaf shall hear. Jesus delivered many people from the devil, evil spirits, and demons. This is confrontation and destruction of the works of Satan and Satan's kingdom.

When Jesus died, he rose from the dead and took away the keys of Death and Hell from satan. Jesus took away all Satan's power and authority. God gave his son Jesus all authority and power.

When Jesus died, Jesus was raised from the dead, ascended into heaven, and placed at the father's right hand; Jesus was given all authority and power in heaven, on the earth, and under the earth.

Jesus said whoever believes in me shall never die but have everlasting life. They have passed out of death into life, and whoever believes in me shall have the right to be a Child of God.

Jesus took back the authority and power that Satan stole from Adam.

Jesus gave us the keys of the kingdom so that whatever we bind on earth will be bound in heaven, and whatever we lose on earth will be loosed in heaven.

Jesus gave Christians the power to do the works that he did.

Jesus said, whoever believes in me shall do the works that I do and even greater works.

It says that his shadow healed the sick as Peter walked along the street.

Jesus called the twelve disciples and gave them power and authority over all demons to cure sickness and disease.

Jesus sent out the seventy, and they returned rejoicing and saying, "Lord, even the demons are subject to us in Your name. Jesus said, "I saw Satan fall like lightning from heaven."

Is the church today seeing satan fall like lightning from heaven? If not, we need to ask the Holy Spirit what we need to do so we can defeat Satan's kingdom.

We need to see satan fall like lightning from heaven.

REFERENCES

Revelation 1:18

I *am* He who lives, and was dead, and behold. I am alive forevermore. Amen. And I have the **keys** of Hades and Death. (Death and Hell)

Psalm 16:10

For You will not leave my soul in Sheol, Nor will You allow Your Holy One to see **corruption**.

Acts 2:29-33

[29] "Men *and* brethren, let *me* speak freely to you of the patriarch David, that he is both dead and buried, and his tomb is with us to this day. [30] Therefore, being a prophet, and

knowing that God had sworn with an oath to him that of the fruit of his body, [I]according to the flesh, He would raise the Christ to sit on his throne, ³¹ he, foreseeing this, spoke concerning the resurrection of the Christ, that His soul was not left in Hades, nor did His flesh see corruption. ³² This Jesus God has raised, of which we are all witnesses. ³³ Therefore being exalted [j]to the right hand of God, and having received from the Father the promise of the Holy Spirit, He poured out this which you now see and hear.

Psalm 106:10-16

¹⁰ Those who sat in darkness and the shadow of death, Bound[b] in affliction and irons— ¹¹ Because they rebelled against the words of

God, And [c]despised the counsel of the Highest, ¹² Therefore He brought down their heart with labor; They fell, and *there was* none to help. ¹³ Then they cried out to the Lord in their trouble, *And* He saved them out of their distresses. ¹⁴ He brought them out of darkness and the shadow of death, And broke their chains into pieces. ¹⁵ Oh, that *men* would give thanks to the Lord *for* His goodness, And *for* His wonderful works to the children of men! ¹⁶ For He has broken the gates of bronze, And cut the bars of iron in two.

CHAPTER 12

THE WAY INTO PARADISE THE GARDEN OF EDEN HAS NOW BEEN OPENED BY JESUS (BELIEVERS ARE GIVEN A NEW SPIRIT—THEY ARE A NEW CREATION)

When Jesus was on the cross, he said to the thief next to him that today he would be with him in paradise. The thief on the cross did not go down to death but was taken straight to paradise.

Before Jesus, all the people of Israel (saints) who died went down into death.

When Adam and Eve sinned in the Garden of Eden, God placed an angel with a flaming sword at the entrance into paradise so that man / Adam could not go back into paradise but had to go down into death when they died.

All the people of Israel that died after Adam went down to death.

After his crucifixion, Jesus went down to death and took away from satan the keys to death and hell.

Jesus took the keys of Death and Hell off Satan and the Angel of death.

When John went to heaven in the book of Revelations, Jesus said to John, "Behold, I have the keys to Death and Hell."

When Jesus was crucified and died, Jesus went down into Death and Hell. Jesus then led the people of Israel and those who believed in him out of death and into Paradise. Jesus restored God's original plan that Adam should live in Paradise (Garden of Eden) and continually have fellowship with God.

This is confirmed in the Psalms and many scriptures throughout the Bible. The purpose of Jesus was to restore all things and restore the authority that Satan had stolen from Adam and Mankind.

Jesus now had three types of Authority, one as the Son of Man, one as the Son of God, and one as the Word of God. When Jesus rose from the dead, there was an earthquake, and people in Jerusalem were raised from the dead and went into the City of Jerusalem and spoke to many people. This signified that the people who belonged to Jesus were now raised from the dead and led into the Garden of Eden.

These people went into the city and gave a testimony that Jesus had appeared in death, Taken control of death and led the people of Israel out of death into the land of Paradise. Jesus said he came to destroy Satan's works, including Death.

Under the inspiration of the Holy Spirit, David saw a time when his flesh would not see corruption, and he would be resurrected and placed in the Garden of Eden and the Kingdom of God's presence. All believers who die in Christ are resting in Paradise, awaiting the second coming of Christ and the Final Judgement of people who do not believe in Jesus. The Believers in Jesus Christ have already passed out of Judgement, and their spirit has access to the Holy of Holies thru the blood of Jesus.

Just as the People in Jerusalem were raised in the Body, the people of Israel were raised in soul and body and placed in Paradise. However, their spirit is eternal and is raised and seated in Heavenly Places in Christ Jesus.

People who are not Christians still go down to death and are waiting for the final judgment. If we read the Book of Revelations, we see that there are still some major events before the Final Coming of Jesus and the Day of Judgement.

Believers in Christ have already passed out of Judgement and received the Gift of eternal life. Jesus said he who believes in me will never die and has already passed out of Judgement into eternal life.

REFERENCES

Luke 23:43
And Jesus said to him, "Assuredly, I say to you, today you will be with Me in **Paradise**."

Revelation 2:7
"He who has an ear, let him hear what the Spirit says to the churches. To him who overcomes, I will give to eat from the tree of life, which is amid the **Paradise** of God.'"

Genesis 3:24
So He drove out the man; and He placed cherubim at the east of the

garden of **Eden**, and a flaming sword which turned every way, to guard the way to the tree of life

Matthew 27:51-53
⁵¹ Then, behold, the veil of the temple was torn in two from top to bottom; and the earth quaked, and the rocks were split, ⁵² and the graves were opened, and many bodies of the saints who had fallen asleep were raised; ⁵³ and coming out of the graves after His resurrection, they went into the holy city and appeared to many.

CHAPTER 13

Believers in Jesus have Everlasting Life
They have passed out of Judgement

Jesus said God so loved the world that whoever believes in me shall not perish but have eternal life. They have already passed out of judgment into eternal life. Jesus said whoever believes in me, and I give them the right to be a Child of God. The Apostle Paul said there is now no condemnation for those in Christ Jesus. Anyone who can say Jesus is Lord and Saviour belongs to Jesus and has passed from death to Life. No one can say

"Jesus is Lord" except the Holy Spirit. Believers in Jesus have received the Holy Spirit and become a NEW CREATION. Those that the Spirt of God leads are Sons of God. When we give our lives to Jesus, we die to the Law and are under a new law, the law of Grace. Therefore because God's gift of salvation thru his son was a gift, we cannot earn salvation by obeying the Law of Moses. As it is written, cursed is everyone under the law. But we are not cursed because we are no longer under the Law.

Those that believe Jesus is the son of God are given the right to be a Child of God. Those who the Holy Spirit leads are not under the Law. Where there is no Law, there is no sin. There is no condemnation for those in Christ Jesus.

The Circumcision Party tries to take believers back to the Temple System and the Law of Moses. If we try to become righteous by our works, we negate the Crucifixion of Jesus. If we can make ourselves Holy and earn the Gift of

Eternal Life, what is the Point of Jesus' Sacrifice and Crucifixion?

This is satan's plan that we should continually strive for but never attain Holiness and Righteousness. Satan's plan is a masterstroke; a person gives their life to Jesus, is immediately set free and delivered into the fullness of the Kingdom of God, and then Joins a Church of the Circumcision Party and is immediately put back into Bondage.

This is the same as the people of Israel who were delivered from Egypt. While Moses was up on the Mountain with God, they asked Aaron to make them a God of Egypt to lead them and to take them back to Egypt.

Many Churches today are being run by the Circumcision Party, putting people back in Bondage and leading them back to Egypt.

I ask any believer why would you want to go back to Egypt, back into Bondage.

Just as in times past, and years ago, the Circumcision Party killed those that the Spirit of

God leads. Spiritual Matters and Revelation cannot be understood by the rational thinking mind or by reading the Bible. The Scribes and Pharisees continually read and searched the scriptures but still hated and murdered Jesus.

In some churches, things have not changed, and the Temple Worship continues but with a slightly more palatable format.

Just as in times past, Judas Iscariot betrayed Jesus, so many people today love to betray the true Spiritual Believers to the Church Authorities.

In a sense, one could say that Judas Iscariot is alive and well and hiding in Churches.

We have already passed from death to Life. As Paul said, Our Spirit is made alive and seated in Heavenly Places.

Every person who believes in Jesus is given the right to be a Priest and King. Those that the Spirt of God leads are Sons of God. Those that the Spirit of God leads are not under the Law. There is now No Condemnation for those in Christ Jesus.

REFERENCES

John 1:10-13

[10] He was in the world, and the world was made through Him, and the world did not know Him. [11] He came to His [c]own, and His [d]own did not receive Him. [12] But as many as received Him, to them He gave the [e]right to become children of God, to those who believe in His name: [13] who were born, not of blood, nor the will of the flesh, nor the will of man, but of God.

Romans 3:21-26
God's Righteousness Through Faith

²¹ But now the righteousness of God apart from the law is revealed, being witnessed by the Law and the Prophets, ²² even the righteousness of God, through faith in Jesus Christ, to all [f]and on all who believe. For there is no difference; ²³ for all have sinned and fall short of the glory of God, ²⁴ being justified [g]freely by His grace through the redemption that is in Christ Jesus, ²⁵ whom God set forth *as* a [h]propitiation by His blood, through faith, to demonstrate His righteousness, because in His forbearance God had passed over the sins that were previously committed, ²⁶ to demonstrate at present His righteousness, that He might be just and the justifier of the one who has faith in Jesus.

CHAPTER 14

The Simple Gift of Eternal Life

Before the conclusion of "The Temple Veil was Torn in Two" in Ch 16, I feel led to share a very simple message from God. God's Message to mankind for eternal life or eternal death is not complicated.

It can be summarized by one single Line. If you believe that Jesus is the Son of God, you are acceptable to God, or to put this differently. If you accept Jesus as your Lord and Saviour, you will receive Eternal Life.

What does this mean?

You will receive the gift of becoming a Child of God. A Child of God has the right to live eternally in the presence of God the Father.

Eternal Life is Life in the presence of Jesus forever.

Eternal Death is separation from the presence of Jesus. This is why it is so important to believe in Jesus now because the decision in this life affects our life in eternity.

Therefore, we need to decide to believe in Jesus to go to heaven and receive eternal life.

God has decided that everything ever made in Heaven and Earth will come under the authority of his son Jesus. The whole of creation is to be submitted to the Kingship of Jesus. Jesus' Title was "The King of the Jews" when he was crucified.

God decided that Jesus, his Son, would become the King and Ruler of the Whole Earth and the Whole of Creation for eternity.

Jesus has become the King of all creation and all people in Heaven, Earth, and under the Earth.

To receive eternal life, God has decided that you have to believe that Jesus is the Son of God and has been appointed as the King of God's Kingdom.

This means we must submit to the Authority of Jesus as a King.

On the day of Judgement, there will only be one test.

Do you believe that Jesus is the Son of God and the King of Heaven and Earth???

Before you die on this earth, you have to decide on your answer.

> Yes—you receive eternal life in a place where Jesus is King
>
> No—you receive eternal death in a place where Satan is King.
>
> Yes—you want to live in a place of eternal perfection
>
> No—you want to live in a place of eternal imperfection with immense suffering and torment.

God is establishing the Kingdom of Heaven over which Jesus will reign as the King. The Kingdom of Heaven will come down and become a New Heaven and a New Earth. The Mount of Olives will split in two, and the Heavenly City Jerusalem will come down on the plane formed between the two halves of the Mount of Olives.

We need to look back in history to understand what a Kingdom means. For example, in Medieval Times, when a King died, a New King was appointed as the Ruler of the Country, and every subject had to swear allegiance to the New King.

Each Subject is asked a question :

Do you swear Allegiance to the New King?

Yes—You become a member of the New Kingdom

No—You are executed and put to death as a traitor because you rejected the King.

There is no in-between state

Either you live, or you die.

When the King asks, "Are you going to swear Allegiance to me?"

There is no debate with the King about:

Well, what new laws are you going to introduce?

Well, what new taxes am I going to pay?

Well, will I benefit from my Alliance with this New King?

The only choice is to Swear Allegiance to Jesus and Live or Deny Jesus and Die.

I humbly beg you and urge you to swear Allegiance to Jesus right now and Live. Because if you cannot say Jesus is your Lord and Saviour, you will not go to Heaven on the Day of Judgement. I cannot say it more clearly.

Yes, Jesus Loves you, paid the sacrifice for your sins and wants you to receive eternal life. Because of God's rules, you will not go to Heaven if you cannot say Jesus is your Lord and Saviour.

As the Apostle Paul said," Test every Spirit, every spirit that cannot say Jesus is Lord is not from God" (That means is not part of God's Kingdom but part of satins kingdom)

The Old King is satan, and he is currently the ruler of the Earth. The New King is Jesus, the new coming King and Ruler of the Whole Heaven and Earth.

Therefore, choose who you will serve?

I am amazed at Churches that seem to think they can bargain with God.

They say, "We believe in Jesus but obey the Law of Moses. "Therefore, because we obey the Law of Moses and are Holy, Righteous, and nice people, we deserve to go to Heaven. God's reply is similar to Jesus:you brood of Vipers, you sons of satan, you liars and Hypocrites, you will never enter my Kingdom because you have rejected my son Jesus.

Some Church Leaders may be going to Hell because they will be judged more harshly than people who do not have learning and understanding. The Leaders of the Church should have known better and have no excuse. Their very complicated Theological Arguments will not save them. Of course, only God knows who is going to Hell because his judgment is perfect, and he judges the motives of people's hearts.

Everyone is only going to be asked one question:

Can you say Jesus is your Lord and Saviour?

No one can say Jesus is Lord except by the Holy Spirit. I speak to many Christians as well as people who are seeking the truth. If their answer to the above question is No, I do not believe in Jesus, Then they cannot enter Heaven and will go down to Hell for eternity.

It is said that just as the Leaders of the Jewish Temple were responsible for the death of nearly the whole Jewish Nation in AD 70 because they rejected Jesus.

So, the Leaders of today's Churches are responsible for the deaths of many millions of People because they gave them the False Gospel, and they are responsible for the blood of the people.

Paul said, "The people who taught a false Gospel were cursed." Therefore, right now, people need to declare that they believe in Jesus as the son of God and receive Eternal Life.

When you die, it is too late to stand before God because you have rejected his son Jesus. It is written, "God so loved the world that he gave his only son that whoever believes in him shall have eternal life. But whoever does not believe in his son is condemned already."

When we buy a car, we take out Insurance so we will not suffer a loss. Why would people not take out insurance to ensure they do not suffer an eternal loss.

CHAPTER 15

Scriptures

John 3:16-21

¹⁶ For God so loved the world that He gave His only begotten Son, that whoever believes in Him should not perish but have everlasting life. ¹⁷ For God did not send His Son into the world to condemn the world, but that the world through Him might be saved. ¹⁸ "He who believes in Him

is not condemned; but he who does not believe is condemned already, because he has not believed in the name of the only begotten Son of God. ¹⁹ And this is the condemnation, that the light has come into the world, and men loved darkness rather than light because their deeds were evil. ²⁰ For everyone practicing evil hates the light and does not come to the light, lest his deeds should be exposed. ²¹ But he who does the truth comes to the light, that his deeds may be seen, that they have been done in God."

John 1:10-13

¹⁰ He was in the world, and the world was made through Him, and the world did not know Him. ¹¹ He came to His [c]own, and His [d] own did not receive Him. ¹² But as

many as received Him, to them He gave the [e]right to become children of God, to those who believe in His name: [13] who were born, not of blood, nor the will of the flesh, nor the will of man, but God.

Romans 1:18-32

[18] For the wrath of God is revealed from heaven against all ungodliness and unrighteousness of men, who [d]suppress the truth in unrighteousness, [19] because what may be known of God is [e]manifest [f]in them, for God has shown *it* to them. [20] For since the creation of the world His invisible *attributes* are seen, being understood by the things that are made, *even* His eternal power and [g]Godhead, so that they are without excuse, [21] because, although they knew God, they did

not glorify *Him* as God, nor were thankful, but became futile in their thoughts, and their foolish hearts were darkened. ²² Professing to be wise, they became fools, ²³ and changed the glory of the incorruptible God into an image made like [h]corruptible man—and birds and four-footed animals and creeping things. ²⁴ Therefore, God also gave them up to uncleanness, in the lusts of their hearts, to dishonor their bodies among themselves, ²⁵ who exchanged the truth of God for the lie, and worshiped and served the creature rather than the Creator, who is blessed forever. Amen. ²⁶ For this reason God gave them up to vile passions. For even their [I]women exchanged the natural use for what is against nature. ²⁷ Likewise also the [j]men, leaving the natural use of the [k]woman, burned in their lust for one another, men with men committing what is shameful, and receiving in themselves the penalty of their error which was due.

28 And even as they did not like to retain God in *their* knowledge, God gave them over to a debased mind, to do those things which are not fitting; 29 being filled with all unrighteousness, [l]sexual immorality, wickedness, [m]covetousness, [n]maliciousness; full of envy, murder, strife, deceit, evil-mindedness; *they are* whisperers, 30 backbiters, haters of God, violent, proud, boasters, inventors of evil things, disobedient to parents, 31 [o]undiscerning, untrustworthy, unloving, [p]unforgiving, unmerciful; 32 who, knowing the

righteous judgment of God, that those who practice such things are deserving of death, not only do the same but also approve of those who practice them.

CONCLUSION

The Gospel Message is very simple and two-fold:

1. If you believe that Jesus is the Son of God, you will receive the gift of eternal life.

You receive the Right to be a Child of God. You receive the Right to enter the Kingdom of God

2. Jesus' sacrifice has paid the price for the whole world's sins.

There is no longer a requirement to sacrifice for the forgiveness of sins, Jesus' sacrifice was a once for all sacrifice never to be repeated. Therefore, God is no no-longer going to judge us according to our sins, We judge ourselves by one simple statement—Do we believe that Jesus is the son of God. Jesus said that the Holy Spirit would convict the world of sin—which is sin that they have not believed in the one and only Son of God.

This Gospel message that God gave mankind is one of the most amazing things ever happening in the History of Mankind. Gospel means Good News. The old prophets said, "How beautiful upon the mountains are the feet of him that brings Good News."

I believe the Gospel Message is also the most misunderstood in the whole of Human History. To our natural mind and the physical world that we see, It is difficult to see how this message could make any sense.

To some people, the message is not at all clear and difficult to understand.

This can be because sometimes the Pastors, Priests, and Theologians who teach the message do not have an understanding of the message they teach. They have made the teaching of the message too complicated.

The message has been made so simple that even a child can understand it, Even the simplest person of low intelligence can understand it. You do not need to have a degree in Theology to teach the message because even simple fishers with no education were the first people Jesus asked to teach this message.

That is because the message is not received in our intellect but in our hearts. It is a message of Love based on the relationship that God is our Father, and we are his children.

The message is so simple that I will repeat it:If you believe that Jesus is the Son of God, you will receive the gift of eternal life. You receive the Right to be a Child of God.

Therefore, God is no no-longer going to judge us according to our sins, we judge ourselves by one simple statement—Do we believe that Jesus is the son of God.

The message can be expanded based on the above statements, but the basic message is unchanged, even when you add a lot of information and detail.

No earthly Father wants to punish his Children. Therefore God made away so that His Human Children could escape punishment, "The Way" is opened by the Heavenly Son of God taking their place and being punished instead of the Earthly Human Children. But there is so much more. It is the relationship with Jesus that is important. We need such a close relationship with Jesus that he calls us friends.

Jesus said, "I am the Way, the Truth and the Life. There is no other way to the father except thru me".

In the Old Temple System, a lamb was sacrificed once a year for the sins of the Children of Israel. Sins are another way of saying we have disobeyed God and not done what he has asked us to do.

Similar to Children who disobey their earthly Mothers and Fathers. One of God's rules is to Honour and Obey your Fathers and Mothers. (Respect their rules)

The Blood of the Lamb was a once-a-year payment for the Sins of Israel. Or the Blood took the place of the sins. The Sacrificial Lamb was considered Holy because its blood was offered on the Altar. It could be considered that God arranged a transaction whereby the sins of Israel were canceled once a year, and the people of Israel became Holy. (Righteous and without Sins)

When Jesus took the place of the Lamb, Jesus' blood was offered for our sins, and we became Holy thru the blood of Jesus.

God exchanged our sinful nature for Jesus' Holy and Righteous Nature. When that exchange took place, we entered into a New Covenant. Thru the covering of the Blood of Jesus, we became Holy and Righteous, and God said he would remember our sins no more.

We exchanged our carnal, sinful nature for the Holy and Righteous nature of Jesus.

An Earthly Priest was not allowed to enter the Holy of Holies without wearing special garments and going thru a ritual of Sanctification and Purification. He needed to be purified from his sins thru the Blood of the Lamb.

If the Earthly Priest did not follow the Sanctification Process properly when he went into the Holy of Holies, he instantly died. He died because God cannot look at Sin and our sinful nature. As it is written, no man may look on the face of God and Live. Moses in the flesh was only allowed to look after God had passed him by.

So, to summarize the full revelation of the events that happened when the Temple Veil was Torn in two—Refer Summary from the Introduction

Summary:

- The Veil of the Temple being Torn in Two represents:
- The Body and Flesh of Jesus are being torn for us.
- End of the "Old Covenant" - Start of the "New Covenant"
- End of Temple System—Start of Jesus / Holy Spirit Ministry—Jesus completed his work
- End of the Law of Moses - Start of God's Law of Grace (Jesus fulfilled the Law)
- End of the Aaronic Priesthood—Start of the Melchizedek Priesthood (Jesus)
- (A change of Law results in a change in Priesthood)
- Aaronic Priesthood was human and temporary–Melchizedek Priesthood is spiritual and eternal
- End of each Human High Priest who dies—Start of Jesus as the eternal High Priest

- End of Lamb of Sacrifice each year—Jesus is the once-only Sacrifice for Forgiveness of Sins
- Jesus' body is the Veil that was torn to forgive sins.
- End of High Priest placing Blood for Forgiveness of Sins on the mercy seat each year
- (Jesus' Blood is the once for all perfect sacrifice for the forgiveness of sins)
- End of High Priest Pronouncing forgiveness of sins thru Sacrifice of the Lamb
- (Belief in Jesus, his Blood, and Baptism is the only way to receive forgiveness of sins)
- End of Temple Priestly Rituals and Duties—Holy Spirit is now in charge of the church.
- End of the Earthly Holy Place—We can enter the Heavenly Holy Place by the blood of Jesus

- End of the High Priest as Mediator between Man and God
- (Believers now have direct access—The Holy Spirit dwells within us)
- (Our body is the Temple of the Holy Spirit)
- End of Satan's reign—Jesus took away the keys of death and hell.
- (Jesus destroyed the works of satan - gave us the power to defeat all the works of the enemy)
- The way into Paradise / Garden of Eden has now been opened by Jesus
- (Believers are given a New Spirit—they are a New Creation)
- For those who believe in Jesus—Everlasting Life—we have passed out of Judgement
- Our Spirit is made alive and seated in Heavenly Places
- Jesus is King and Priest (Never before has these two Offices been held by one person—Jesus)

- Every person who believes in Jesus is given the right to be a Priest and King
- Circumcision Party tries to take believers back to the Temple System and the Law of Moses
- (If we try to become righteous on our own, we negate the Crucifixion of Jesus)
- Circumcision Party tries to control believers by applying the Law of Moses
- (They make themselves the Judge over believers, they replace God)
- Those that the Spirt of God leads are Sons of God
- Those that believe Jesus is the son of God are given the right to be a Child of God
- Those who the Holy Spirit leads are not under the Law
- Where there is no Law, there is no sin
- There is now no condemnation for those in Christ Jesus

Bonus 1: We are Called by God but come to a Comfortable Place we no Longer Obey God and Turn to Idols

Tarah was the Father of Abraham. God called Tarah and said, "Leave your Family and Relatives and go to the Land I will show you. So Tarah left his Family and relatives, came to Haram, and stopped there.

Tarah saw that Haram was a Good Place where he could be comfortable. Tarah became so comfortable in Haram that he did not travel any further but stayed in Haram all his life. Tarah stopped obeying God, and Tarah's' Household, after some time, eventually turned to their household gods and worshipped Idols.

After many years God called Abram (Abraham) Tarah's Son and told him to leave his Father's House and travel to the Land God would show him. Abraham Obeyed God and traveled until he came to Canaan. God Blessed Abraham, and Abraham dwelt in the Land of Canaan that God gave to Abraham and his descendants.

Some years later, Isaac sent Jacob back to the House of Tarah to Labuan in Padano Aram to get himself a wife from Labuan, who was now the head of the Tarah's Household. Jacob married Leah and Rachel. When Jacob left Labuan, Rachel stole Labuan's Household gods and Idols.

This story suggests that Tarah's Household turned away from worshipping God to worshipping other gods and Idols. The story above is symbolic for Christians today. God calls many Christians, they start by Obeying God. Then they come to a place that is Good and Comfortable. They stay there and do not Journey any further. They stop obeying and listening to God. They do not receive the full blessing that God has prepared for them; they are,e so Comfortable in this Good Place that they start to forget about God and eventually raise Idolsplace God.

The Idols seem Good, but they have replaced God as the most important thing in our lives. The Idol can be our Husband/Wife and Family, our Job and Financial Security, our Health, Sports, Drug Addiction, Alcohol, Sexual Addiction, Politics, or other r sorts of Idols. As we become Good and Comfortable and secure, we tend to depend less and less on God, weer call on God when we have an emergency.

I have noticed in Australia, many Christians focus on Sports like Footie. (Australian Rules) One weekend there was a Footie Grand Final, The Focus of the Church Meeting as it started was the Footie Final, as the Priest Discussed this the Laptop Stopped working, the Sound System went off, the Overhead Projector went off, The servant and ice were held up for over half an hour while the Priests' Husband went to get a back-up Laptop from Home and then set up the Laptop in the Church so the service could re-start. God is not pleased when we set up an Idol in the Church and will warn us. If we are wise, we will listen to God's warning, turn away from the Idol, and turn back to obey God's Call.

Bonus 2: Putting our trust in a Man and not in God

REFER EXODTO US CHAPTER 32:

When God delivered Israel out of Egypt by the hand of Moses, the people's reaction was very interesting. The People put their trust in Moses rather than in God. When Israel was in the desert, Moses went up to Mount Sinai to speak to God. Moses was a long time with God, so after some time, the People said to Aaron," Where is this Moses that brought us out of Egypt? What has become of him? Come make us gods that shall go before us".

Israel's focus on a man and not on God resulted in Aaron trying to please and placate the people. Aaron made them a Gold Calf as an Idol and presented it to the people., Then the people said, "This is your god O Israel that brought you out of Egypt."

The Gold Calf represented going back to Egypt and being protected by the gods of Egypt. God was not impressed and told Moses that the people had corrupted themselves. Israel placed their trust in Moses instead of God, and this resulted in several problems,

1. They did not Trust in God
2. They trusted in the Leader Moses
3. When they felt the leader had let them down, they created an Idol and started worshipping the Idol—they wanted to go back to Egypt
4. They turned away from God
5. They rose to play—I believe this means they had promiscuous sexual relations.
6. Moses wanted to destroy Israel and make it a great nation.

Today this story represents the Church and the people in the Church. If the people trust God and have a relationship with Jesus, everything is fine. If the people put their trust in the Church and the Pastor, then this will result in several problems:

1. The people will not fully trust in God
2. The people will trust in the Church and the Pastor
3. If there is a problem with the Church and Pastor, they will start creating Idols and want to go back to Egypt (The World System)
4. The people will turn away from God
5. The People will start going back to their old worldly ways of Immorality and Addiction

The people will become increasingly dependent on the world and sophisticated systems. They will try and use Politics to fix Problems, They will start to descend into Sexual Immorality, Drug Addiction, Alcohol Addiction, Family Breakdowns, etc.

If Christians don't want to go backward and descend into the depths of the world, then they need to make God First and Church and Pastor second. They need to make their relationship with Jesus and The Holy Spirit the most important thing in their life.

We are in the middle of a war with Satan, and he will do everything in his power to destroy Christians who are Powerful because of their relationship with Christ.

When I talk to Christians, I am surprised that many of them do not seem to realize that we are in a war with the Kingdom of Satan.

Just like when God told Israel he was giving them the land of Canaan, they still had to fight to possess the Land and destroy Giants.

Today, God has given us Victory thru the Blood of Jesus. We have been given the Land, we still have to fight to possess the Land and destroy Giants.

We are the Ground Troops on the Earth that Jesus uses to defeat the Kingdom of satan. Our warfare is not carnal but against spiritual wickedness in heavenly places. In the First Church, the Holy Spirit instructed the believers to go to certain places and carry out certain actions. The Holy Spirit instructed the church to send out Paul and Barnabas.

We need to be the hands and feet, eyes and ears and mouth of the army of God on the earth.

We need to pray as the Holy Spirit leads us. Every Christian has a role to perform to advance the Kingdom of God on Earth.

Paul made a great sacrifice to advance the Kingdom of God and Evangelise most of the Known World at that time. Many of the First Apostles and believers also made great sacrifices.

Are we not willing to at least do something to advance the Kingdom of God where we live. All we need to do is ask the Holy Spirit what he wants us to do and obey the leading of the Holy Spirit? I hear churches many times praying for Revival? They will not get it because they are not willing to Obey the Leading of the Holy Spirit.

Instead, the Churches have a large number of Programs or pet Theological Church Growth Ideas. The people in the Church say, "Oh No, I couldn't possibly go out and speak to people about Jesus." This type of Church will die as no new members will be added to their number. I have personal experience of watching these churches shut down. It is not immediate and can sometimes take 10 to 20 years. The best Church Growth Strategy is based on the Book of Acts.

However, they will not allow the Holy Spirit to direct the meetings, evangelism, or Healings and Miracles.

Sometimes they even say these things passed away with the first Apostles. The general public sees the church as Powerless and not displaying any unusual Spiritual Power, while the Church is not displaying God's Power, there will not be a revival. While the Church is disobedient to the leading of the Holy Spirit, there will not be a Revival. Understand that sometimes Revival is not instant and can take a number of years, however, there will not be any revival until someone starts obeying the Holy Spirit. It may only need one Evan Roberts or William Seymour to start a Revival. Are you going to be the one God uses to bless maybe 100,000 people in 6 months or a whole nation in 2 Years, as in the Welsh Revival? Once the Holy Spirit starts to work through one person, many other people join in as the Holy Spirit comes upon them, and then there is exponential growth.

I pray that everyone will obey the Leading of the Holy Spirit so that we may have Revival. Revival in our hearts and Revival in the Church. Amen.

ABOUT THE AUTHOR

Michael Shenton was brought up in Swansea, UK, in a council house estate. He originally joined the Welsh Church of England when he was 4 years old until he was approximately 14 years old.

Michael was in the Church Choir and a Server at Church Communion / Evensong for 4 years. He moved to Bunbury, WA, in 1987 and later became a member of the Anglican Church Healing Ministry Team run by Joe Hopkins. While in the ministry, Michael saw many healings and minor miracles during that time.

In 1999, God called Michael to start a Revival at St. Nicholas Church Australind, WA. He received his Prophetic Office from Paul Cain and his Apostolic Office from John Wimber.

Michael's ministry is like Paul to Timothy. He prays for people to receive the gifts of the Holy Spirit and then prays for their ministry to be in God's providence continually. He also trains and mentors the members and supports them in their ministry's needs.

Michael is not and has never been interested in the gains of his own ministry but is rather more interested in supporting and uplifting others.

Michael's ministry is very simple—he listens to the Holy Spirit and carries out whatever the Holy Spirit enlightens him to do.

Personally, Michael had met Jesus several times, not in a vision but face-to-face. Also, he had been to Heaven approximately over 30 times. This meeting with Jesus and being taken to Heaven is available to anyone, same with John and Paul, who met Jesus and were taken to

Heaven, and Michael does not see that he is any different from them.

Despite the rare opportunity of witnessing and feeling God, Michael still sees himself as no one special. He thinks anyone can do what he does if they have unwavering faith in God and a formidable relationship with Him.

Michael hopes that his experiences with God encourage you to never be afraid in seeking and creating your spiritual journey with Him.

www.ingramcontent.com/pod-product-compliance
Lightning Source LLC
Chambersburg PA
CBHW061759070526
44586CB00023B/2639